AUTHENTIC
LEADERSHIP

Musings on Supplementing Skills and Happiness

Jagat Singh Bisht

Dedicated to
The NZ Leadership Programme
Class of 2021

CONTENTS

Often your tasks will be many,

And more than you think you can do.

Often the road will be rugged

And the hills insurmountable, too.

But always remember, the hills ahead

Are never as steep as they seem,

And with Faith in your heart start upward

And climb 'Til you reach your dream.

Helen Steiner Rice

PROLOGUE

ENHANCING LEADERSHIP SKILLS

"A good life
is characterized by
complete absorption
in what one does."
Jeanne Nakamura
and Mihaly Csikszentmihalyi

Our daughter-in-law, Sneha, shared, with a sense of visible pride, that she would be participating in a unique programme – The New Zealand Leadership Programme – along with a group of mid-career, senior and community leaders.
She said that the programme will be delivered through seven immersive and experiential retreats

over a period of nine months. Apart from enhancing personal leadership skills, it envisages to catalyse participants' sense of purpose and build vision for a more hopeful future for Aotearoa.

I was sanguine that she is in for a psychologically rich experience that will bring deep learning and immense joy.

I also felt nostalgic about the times when I groomed young leaders in the State Bank of India as a behavioral science trainer. I realized that the participants must be aware of their intra-personal processes, develop capacity for warm inter-personal relationships, and learn the key skills to be an effective and authentic leader.

It occurred to me to pen down random musings – concepts, ideas and thoughts – for the benefit of leaders and aspiring leaders.

This book is essentially about valuable skills that supplement leadership qualities. It is based on theories and models from behavioral science and positive psychology. It also gives you a new understanding of happiness and well-being and how to flourish in life.

"This is the true joy in life –

being used for a purpose

recognized by yourself

as a mighty one."

George Bernard Shaw

AUTHENTIC LEADER

PRUDENCE, TEMPERANCE, JUSTICE AND FORTITUDE

"Authentic leaders are not born that way. Many people have natural leadership gifts, but they have to develop them fully to become outstanding leaders. Authentic leaders use their natural abilities, but they also recognize their shortcomings and work hard to overcome them. They lead with purpose, meaning, and values. They build enduring relationships with people. Others follow them because they know where they stand. They are consistent and self-disciplined. When their principles are tested, they refuse to compromise. Authentic leaders are dedicated to developing themselves because they know that becoming a leader takes a lifetime of personal growth."

Bill George

T he most effective and satisfied leaders are those who behave in a genuine and authentic manner which requires high levels of personal awareness and contact with what is presently happening materially, emotionally and behaviorally in the here and now.

An authentic leader is self-aware, emotionally intelligent, creative, stress-free, and takes judicious decisions.

An authentic leader is genuine, ethical, fair-minded, mission driven, and focussed on the long-term.

An authentic leader believes in open and honest communication.

The ancient Greek philosophers emphasized upon four key virtues: prudence, temperance, justice and fortitude. These are known as the *cardinal virtues*.

Prudence: Practical wisdom. Ability to consider all possible courses of action and arrive at a judicious decision.

Justice: Fair-mindedness in dealing with people.

Fortitude: Courage to do the right things.

Temperance: Moderation in desires, emotional balance and self-control.

An authentic leader needs the four virtues in order to lead in a just and good manner, as developing these virtues results in improving the inner-self and relationships with people.

There have been several authentic leaders in the history of mankind. They not only excelled in their respective fields but set an example of authentic leadership before the world. To name just a few of them:

Abraham Lincoln

Mahatma Gandhi

Martin Luther King Jr.

J. R. D. Tata

Warren Buffet

The Buddha.

"Authentic leadership is leading adaptively from your core,

choosing who you're most inspired to be

to serve the greatest good in this moment."

Henna Inam

SUPPLEMENTING SKILLS

FROM SELF-AWARENESS TO SUPER EFFECTIVENESS

"We can lift ourselves

out of ignorance,

we can find ourselves

as creatures of excellence

and intelligence and skill.

We can be free!

We can learn to fly!"

Richard Bach

T he fundamental building blocks of authentic leadership are self-awareness and self-management. If you know yourself, understand your core self, and have control over your impulses, along with autonomy to choose a suitable response to a stimulus, you have the potential to be an authentic leader.

We all have within us a child, an adult, and a parent. This becomes apparent when we respond differently to different situations – exhibiting fear, playfulness, balance, self-control, hatred, love, and compassion.

Sometimes we are childlike – full of feelings and emotions – laughing, crying, jumping, shouting, and screaming. At times we behave like an adult – fully aware and organized – oriented to the current reality. On other occasions, we tend to be like parents – critical and prejudicial – and often nurturing too!

Every state of mind is equally important and there is a time for it. There is a time to work and a time to play, a time to laugh and a time to cry, and a time to speak and a time to be silent.

We are all born free. We have the potential to be winners. We have a right to be self-determining. An authentic person experiences self-reality by knowing, being, and becoming a credible, responsive person.

Autonomy is a human birthright. Being autonomous means being self-governing and determining one's own destiny. A slave can never be happy. A slave can never flourish.

According to Stephen Covey, "Every human has four endowments – self-awareness, conscience, independent will and creative freedom. These give us the ultimate human freedom. These give us the power to choose, to respond, and to change."

We must begin by taking responsibility for our own actions and feelings. A close look at intra-personal processes must be our ongoing endeavour. We must also learn to throw off patterns that are irrelevant and inappropriate to living in the here and now.

The litmus test of a truly autonomous person lies hidden in three fundamental capacities – awareness, spontaneity, and intimacy.

Awareness is knowing what is happening now. An autonomous person is aware. His body and mind are in unison in the here and now. It is not that the body is physically present somewhere and the mind is wandering elsewhere.

One must not only be fully present but also fully aware of the situation, surroundings, and feelings of self and others. The decisions taken must depend upon the facts of the situation and not on some pre-conceived notions. Prejudices from the past must not impact actions in the present.

An autonomous person looks objectively at the situation in the present, listens attentively, seeks clarifications to arrive at a deeper understanding of the situation, and arrives at a balanced decision without being influenced by opinions.

One must be in touch with one's feelings and sensations in the body. If you are tense, your breath is shallow. You can relax by taking a few deep breaths and exhaling in a relaxed manner. That will help you clear your mind and make a better decision.

Always listen to the other person with empathy, do not interrupt, and ask questions that help you understand the person in the right perspective. Do not form opinions about the person based on what you have been told earlier. Keep your mind open, make your own observations, and arrive at your conclusions based on the facts before you.

You must be fully present, fully mindful. Do not let your attention wander hither and thither. Let past prejudices and opinions not influence you. Be your own witness. Decide on your own based on the merits of the case. Take full responsibility of the decision taken by you. Be honest and upright.

Sometimes our parental influences crop up to affect our decisions or the playful child contaminates our thinking. One must be vigilant and must be in the right frame of mind, always fully aware, to make the right decisions in the here and now.

You must have the spontaneity to choose from a whole range of behaviour that the child, adult, and parent, residing within you, prompt you to adopt. Your decisions must not always be along the pre-decided patterns that you have been accustomed to witnessing for ages.

Spontaneity denotes choosing the right actions from a wide range of possibilities. You must choose the option that you find appropriate, as per your inner voice, and accept full responsibility for the decision. Let not your inner child or parent influence you, do not be a victim of confusing voices from the past. Be analytical, choose what you find appropriate, and feel relaxed.

If you arrive at free and independent decisions, without being swayed by feelings and prejudices, you will not experience stress. You will be happy. Spontaneity helps you to be autonomous and take control of your destiny.

An autonomous person is spontaneous and flexible – not rigid and impulsive. The person is free despite basic instincts or drives, free despite inherited characteristics and environmental influences. An autonomous person can be realistic and choose from the entire spectrum of behaviour appropriate to the situation.

Intimacy is expressing feelings of warmth, tenderness, and closeness toward others. One must shed masks and old programming, if any, and be warm toward people. One should not be sarcastic or play games with people. One should learn to let go and develop a capacity for intimacy.

People moving toward autonomy expand their personal capacities for awareness, spontaneity, and intimacy. Once you are open and have no conflicting voices within, you are in full control. There is no tension. You feel happy and relaxed.

"It takes courage to be a real winner – not a winner in the sense of beating out someone else by always insisting on coming out on top – but a winner at responding to life. It takes courage to experience the freedom that comes with autonomy, courage to accept intimacy and directly encounter other persons, courage to take a stand in an unpopular cause, courage to choose authenticity over approval and to choose it again and again, courage to accept the responsibility for your own choices, and, indeed, courage to be the very unique person you really are."

Muriel James and Dorothy Jongeward

People skills

Inter-personal relationships are crucial building blocks for authentic leadership. Leaders lead people and their relationships with them have a direct bearing on their success or failure as a leader. If you trust people fully and enable them to perform, they will never let you down. Technical competence has its own importance, but people skills ultimately determine your leadership quotient.

The primary source of joy, for most people, is other people. You can make a person happy and at ease by having a satisfactory relationship. Recognition of identity and attention are basic to human existence and lack of warmth can wither a person.

Interpersonal relations involve understanding of the 'how' and 'why' of relationships and the impact these have on individuals. One must appreciate the compulsions that make people act in a given manner.

People's behaviour in interpersonal relationships is based on three dimensions - inclusion, control and affection/openness.

Inclusion is acceptance or rejection by others, control

is having influence over other people and affection/ openness is the degree to which one is comfortable sharing one's thought and feelings with others.

Each of these three dimensions of behaviour have two manifestations – expressed and wanted.

Expressed behaviour indicates how w behave toward others and wanted behaviour indicates how we want others to behave toward us.

An authentic leader makes people feel included and belonging, with a feeling of togetherness and companionship. She interacts with people paying full attention and interest giving due recognition and acknowledgement, never giving a sense of exclusion.

Control behaviour refers to the decision-making process between people involving the areas of power, influence and authority. One must not be an 'abdicrat', a person too low on control, or an 'autocrat', a person dominating in the extreme. The ideal is a 'democrat' – a capable, responsible person who feels comfortable giving or not giving orders, as is appropriate for the situation.

Affection/openness behaviour indicates openness between people. Neither an 'underpersonal', nor an 'overpersonal' type of behaviour is desirable in work groups. One must be comfortable in being close and also in being far, capable of giving and receiving affection, in a balanced and graceful 'personal' mode.

An authentic leader brings out the best in others by

building relationships. She treats all team members with respect, warmth and fairness. Those who are less competent than you need your patience and encouragement as well. If you are able to carry your team along, you will be a successful leader.

Time structuring

Leaders are required to plan activities, set goals and prioritize tasks for which they use a planner or appointment calendar. This aspect is the physical management of time.

The activities before you may be defined by two factors – *urgent* and *important*. Imagine a time management matrix with four quadrants:

Urgent and important

Not urgent but important

Urgent but not important

Not urgent and not important.

Quadrant I activities include pressing problems that need immediate action.

Quadrant II includes activities that may not be urgent but are important, such as planning.

Quadrant III includes activities that are urgent but

not important, such as telephonic interruptions and routine meetings.

Quadrant IV includes activities that are neither urgent nor important, like social media and time wasters.

A good leader does not waste time in quadrant II and IV. She understands that quadrant I gets bigger and bigger, if you don't spend time in quadrant II, preparing for eventualities.

It is also essential to understand the psychological dimension of how an individual prefers to spend time. It is known as *time structuring*. People structure their time in six possible ways:

Withdrawal

Rituals

Pastimes

Games

Activity

Intimacy.

One may choose to spend as much time as one finds comfortable in any of the six modes mentioned above.

People may be present physically in a meeting but withdraw psychologically into their fantasy world.

Rituals are stereotyped transactions like exchanging pleasantries and attending social, religious rites and observances.

People also spend a lot of time in pastimes – talking about weather, politics and gossips.

Sometimes people may prefer to play psychological games to structure time.

Activities include essential work and tasks to be performed. Intimacy is the feeling of warmth and affection that we feel towards others.

People spend time in withdrawal, rituals, pastimes, games, activity or intimacy to a lesser or greater extent. If you are aware and inclined, you may structure your time in a more effective and productive manner.

Life positions

The concept of life positions is a way of exploring behaviour in terms of whether people see themselves and others as "OK" or "not OK".

"OK" feelings are feelings of power, capability, well-being, lovableness, and personal worth. "Not OK" feelings are feelings of weakness, incompetence, helplessness, insignificance, anxiety, unworthiness of love, and unworthiness.

Early in life, people adopt a life position based on their experience and feelings about their self-worth and about the worth of others. The child adopts one of these perceptions:

I'm Not OK – You're OK: A person holding this belief assumes that he or she is inferior to others in terms of competence, influence or power.

I'm Not OK, You're Not OK: A person holding this life position believes that he or she is worthless and so are others.

I'm OK, You're Not OK: These persons believe that they cannot rely on anyone else but themselves.

These life positions are developed in the first or second year of life and continue to remain. It is difficult to change one's life position, but not impossible.

As one grows up, one must make a conscious effort to change the life position to a healthy life position:

I'm OK, You're OK: Such people see themselves as interdependent with others and their environment. They are OK and see others as OK too.

Creativity

Making the right decisions is of utmost importance for an authentic leader. The situation may be utterly chaotic and full of confusion at times, but one must not lose patience. There is always a way out. A true leader finds creative solutions to problems.

Let us have a look at one of the creativity tools that may be used for arriving at a conclusion in a perplexing situation:

Imagine you have a collection of six hats of different colours – white, red, black, yellow, green, and blue. These are your tools for arriving at the right decisions in complex life situations.

Think of a problem that you have been facing. The problem is confusing and perplexing. You are finding it difficult to arrive at a solution.

Let us begin solving it in a creative and systematic way:

Begin with wearing the white hat.

The white hat denotes purity. You look only at the pure data. Just information and facts of the case. No opinion, views, or prejudices.

You may write down the problem and all related data on a sheet of paper, or prepare a document on your computer.

Make sure it is pure data, no opinions, or pre-conceived notions.

Take off the white hat and put on the red hat.

The red hat denotes emotions. Only emotions. What you feel. No logic, pure emotions.

Express and go through all the emotions. Your fears, anxieties, and hopes about the case. Whatever you feel. Let the whole range of feelings – positive, neutral, and negative – flow. No justifications needed.

Be as irrational and emotional as you can be.

Take off the red hat and put on the black hat.

The black hat is the devil's advocate. Everything that is wrong and that may go wrong in the case. All the failures, drawbacks, and negatives about the case. The emotional as well as the logical dark side.

Imagine all that can go wrong and the havoc that may be created.

Now, take off the black hat and put on the yellow hat.

Yellow is the colour of sunshine, positivity, and optimism. Look at the brighter side of the problem and list all that is good and full of hope about it.

Look at all the positives and be full of optimism and hope.

Take off the yellow hat and put on the green hat.

Green is the colour of creativity and nature. Be creative. Look at the problem from totally different perspectives. Be creative. Think laterally. Think something new, innovate, and out of the box.

Imagine what no one has ever thought about the problem. Be disruptive in your thinking, not just incremental. Find totally new solutions. Brainstorm to the fullest. Use your whole range of thinking – make use of the entire rainbow.

Now, put down the green hat and put on the blue hat.

Blue is the colour of the sky. It covers everything.

Consider whatever you have thought and felt on wearing all the hats – white, red, black, yellow, and green – and summarize them. You must arrive at a balanced decision, taking everything into consideration. You must weigh all the pros and cons.

Make the ultimate decision. Let there be no doubt in mind. All apprehensions must be given consideration and cleared. Take very single factor into account and arrive at the most comprehensive decision.

Your decision should not be lopsided or taken without considering all possible angles. Let it be all encompassing.

You arrive at the right decision and there is no stress.

This method of arriving at a balanced decision in complex situation has been devised by Edward de Bono and is known as the *Six Thinking Hats*.

Not being able to reach at the right decisions causes stress and anxiety. Knowing how to make the right decisions relieves you of stress. If you have a thinking mind, if you are creative, if you are positive, if you believe in activity, and if you are not afraid to take the right decisions, you will always be happy and stress-free.

Creativity is seeing what others are seeing but thinking something different and innovative. It is doing something in a simpler and better way by making the best use of information you have at a specific time.

The terms *lateral thinking* and *creative thinking* are often used interchangeably. Edward de Bono defines Lateral Thinking as follows:

"You cannot dig a hole in a different place by digging the same hole deeper. Lateral Thinking is for changing concepts and perceptions instead of trying harder with the same concepts and perceptions. In self-organizing information systems, asymmetric patterns are formed. Lateral Thinking is a method for cutting across from one pattern to another."

A number of deliberate formal tools for lateral thinking are available. Creative thinking can be learned as a skill to generate new ideas formally and deliberately whenever you wish.

Lateral thinking is different from the traditional vertical thinking that is linear and logical. Vertical thinking is characterized by a logical analysis with one step following another to arrive at a conclusion.

Creativity can be a useful tool in the hands of a leader in difficult situations where conventional wisdom fails to yield results.

"Man's mind,

stretched to a new idea,

never goes back

to its original dimensions."

Oliver Wendell Holmes

Emotional intelligence

For effective leadership, emotional intelligence counts more than intelligence quotient. Technical competence is a must for leaders but what make the difference are the emotional competencies.

Emotional intelligence is the capacity of recognizing our own feelings and those of others, for motivating ourselves, and for managing emotions well in ourselves and in our relationships.

An emotional competence is a learned capability based on emotional intelligence that results in outstanding performance at work.

The emotional competence framework can be broadly divided into two sets of competencies:

Personal competence: How we manage ourselves.

Social competence: How we manage relationships.

The components of personal competence are:

Self-awareness: Includes emotional awareness, self-assessment and self-confidence.

Self-regulation: Includes self-control, trustworthiness, conscientiousness, adaptability and innovation.

Motivation: Includes achievement drive, commitment, initiative and optimism.

The components of social competence are:

Empathy: Includes understanding others, developing others, service orientation, leveraging diversity and political awareness.

Social skills: Includes influence, communication, conflict management, leadership, change catalyst, building bonds, collaboration and cooperation and team capabilities.

People may be weak in some of the competencies and strong in others. The competencies can be learned, practiced, and strengthened. It may not be practically possible to master all the competencies, but one must strive to develop them on an ongoing basis.

Let us look into these skills one by one:

Emotional awareness is recognizing one's emotions and their impact upon self. One must be able to see what emotion one is feeling at the moment – anger, fear, disgust, shame, sadness, surprise, love or enjoyment. One must analyse why one is feeling in a particular manner and what impact it is having on one's behaviour and performance.

One must possess an accurate *self-assessment* of one's abilities and limitations, strengths and weaknesses. One must continuously learn from own experiences and accept feedback from others positively. One must develop new perspectives and focus on self-development.

An authentic leader has a strong sense of self-worth

and capabilities. She possesses *self-confidence*, shares views transparently and arrives at judicious decisions considering pros and cons. She can sustain pressures and overcome uncertainties.

Self-control is staying calm in difficult circumstances. It is having control over disruptive emotions, thoughts and impulses. One stays composed and thinks clearly despite the turbulence in mind. It does not have a negative impact upon performance and behaviour. One does not lose sight of the goals.

Trustworthiness and conscientiousness are the hallmarks of an authentic leader. One has an impeccable integrity, always acts in an ethical manner and is fully reliable. One is not shy to admit mistakes and take responsibility for the failures.

An authentic leader is always open to *innovation and adaptability*. One listens to new ideas and is willing to make changes in approach to a situation. One is flexible in responding to change.

We must always be in search of excellence and strive to do work in the best possible manner. *Achievement drive* compels one to set high standards of performance and reach goals within stipulated time.

Commitment is aligning with the goals of the organization. One must be clear about the vision, mission and values of the organization and prepared to sacrifice for achieving them.

People having the competence of *initiative and optimism* pursue goals beyond what is expected from them and operate from a position of hope rather than fear of failure. They seize new opportunities and cross all hurdles and obstacles to reach there.

Empathy helps us in *understanding others* – their perspective, thought process and feelings. An authentic leader is able to step into the shoes of others mentally and look at the picture from their viewpoint. Gaining this understanding, it becomes easier to put across the requirement and expectations of the organization.

Mentoring and *developing others* is a primary role of the leader. The team members may be deficient in a competency or unclear about their role in a given situation. A leader must guide them, coach them and prepare them for their role.

Organizations thrive on customer service. Customer orientation is an important competency. *Service orientation* is anticipating, recognizing and meeting customer needs. Customers need attentive listening, quick redressal of their complaints and trusted advice.

True leaders see diversity as opportunity and seek *leveraging diversity* by cultivating opportunities through diverse people. They have the ability to understand and appreciate diverse worldviews, are sensitive to group differences and have the ability to carry along people from varied backgrounds.

Political awareness entails accurate reading of organizational and external realities, key power relationships and socio-political currents. One must have the capability to understand the forces that shape views and actions of clients.

Great leaders know how to win friends and *influence* people. They have persuasive, convincing and presentation skills that can sway decisions of others. They are able to build consensus and support on crucial issues by wielding influential tactics.

Communication skills distinguish great leaders from good leaders. It includes the listening, reading, writing and speaking skills. While listening, body language, expressions and non-verbal cues are significantly important. Reading and writing skills give you the required depth of thought and understanding. Speaking skills, one-to-one and public, encompasses putting across your viewpoint in a clear and concise manner and ensuring that it has the desired impact.

Conflict management involves resolving issues, negotiating and orchestrating win-win solutions. One must accept that mutual conflicts among team members must be suitably and amicably resolved, difficult persons appropriately handled, and potential conflicts addressed. The areas of disagreement should be confronted, not avoided, and diplomatic solutions reached for all disturbing issues.

Leadership is bringing out the best in others. Show them the way by leading from the front. Ignite the hopes and dreams of the team members to share the vision of the organization. Wield the power of ethical leadership having dimensions of legitimacy and permanence. Set goals for others. Inspire, guide, and motivate.

You are the *change catalyst* – inspiring and managing change is your major role. Be a mover and shaker, a change master who stays afloat during difficult times and motivates others. The way one accepts, adapts to and meets the challenge of change is crucial in dealing with change. Make others understand that change is the only constant, ask them to try changing the way they look at things and accept change.

Building bonds, nurturing instrumental relationships and cultivating mutually beneficial relationships is a trait of successful leaders. They build networks of trust, rapport and long-term personal friendship with work associates.

Collaboration and cooperation are the new corporate mantras. Share plans, information and resources. Promote a cordial and conducive climate. Build trust and confidence. Work with others towards shared goals.

Develop *team capabilities* and synergy in pursuing collective goals. A capable team leader fosters qualities like respect, helpfulness, cooperation, commitment and participation among team members.

Negotiation skills

"Your real world is a giant negotiating table, and like it or not, you are a participant. You, as an individual, come into conflict with others: family members, sales clerks, competitors, or entities with impressive names like 'the Establishment' or 'the power structure.' How you handle these encounters can determine not only whether you prosper, but whether you can enjoy a full, pleasurable, satisfying life."

Herb Cohen

Most of us know very little about the art of negotiation. Every negotiation involves three elements:

Information: It always appears that the other side knows more about you and your needs than you know about them and their needs. Proper homework must be done before proceeding to the negotiating table.

Time: Never be under the pressure of time while negotiating. There is always ample time available with you though it may appear that the other side is not facing any constraints about time.

Power: Believe that you wield enough power and authority than the other side.

Some negotiators play the game softly and others play it hard. Soft negotiators place higher value on the feelings and relationships of the bargainers than on the substance of the transactions. Hard negotiators place higher value on the issues or things in the transaction than on the relationships of the bargainers.

The most common mistake that negotiators make is to bargain over *positions* rather than *principles*.

One must focus on issues, not personalities, and try to break out of the position trap.

The best strategy is creatively seeking win-win outcomes. If the underlying interests of both the parties have been identified, creative win-win outcomes can be generated.

Principled negotiation seeks standards outside the will of the negotiators for determination of a fair and wise agreement.

"Win/Win is a frame of mind and heart that constantly seeks mutual benefit in all human transactions. Win/Win means that agreements or solutions are mutually beneficial, mutually satisfying. With a Win/Win solution, all parties feel good about the decision and feel committed to the action plan. Win/Win sees life as a cooperative, not competitive arena. Most people tend to think in terms of dichotomies: strong or weak, hardball or softball, win or lose. But that kind of thinking is fundamentally flawed. It is based on power and position rather than on principle. Win/Win is based on the paradigm that there is plenty for everybody, that one person's success is not achieved at the expense or exclusion of the success of others."

Stephen R. Covey

Leadership

Superior leaders share six sets of common practices:

Establishing a vision

Stimulating people to gain new competencies

Helping people to overcome obstacles

Helping people to overcome failure

Leading by example

Including others in their success.

Successful leaders have the following characteristics:

A belief in their ability to develop the potential of their followers

An ability to establish and communicate goals that are challenging, realistic, and achievable

Positive assumptions about the potential of others

A commitment to excellence and enthusiasm

A focus on the human aspects of the task.

Leaders, who expect their followers to succeed, exert positive influences and obtain extraordinary short-term and long-term results. This is known as the *Pygmalion Effect*.

Leadership is an activity in which leaders influence followers to act in order to attain goals representing the motives, needs, wants, hopes, and expectations of both leaders and followers.

Transactional leadership is based on the principle of exchange – recognizing potential followers' needs and initiating contact in hopes of exchanging one need for another.

Transformational leadership is based on the principle of mutual stimulation and elevation - recognizing potential followers' needs but transcending exchanges and inspiring the followers to higher-order satisfaction of needs such as those related to self-actualization, esteem and belonging.

Teamwork

The migrating Canadian geese, flying in a "V" formation, provide one of the best examples of teamwork in Nature. They expend less energy by flying in a group in v-formation and can fly much longer without feeling tried. High performance teams too enhance their performance by support and synergy.

When the leading goose in the front feels tired, it moves to the back row and another one take its place. The goose at the front faces the maximum air pressure and by moving to the back row finds a place to relax a bit. When the team is performing well, this leadership rotation is smooth and helpful. The responsibility of leadership must be shared and each one given a chance to lead.

The geese constantly honk and encourage each other. Likewise, there must be effective communication and encouragement among team members.

An injured goose is escorted by a couple of geese and looked after till it is required. They then return to the flock and join the formation.

Sometimes a goose may try to go alone, leaving the team formation. It feels a heavy drag and returns to the formation to find comfort and support. It is difficult to achieve tasks alone and becomes easier with group members working and supporting each other.

The lessons learnt from the geese are proper alignment of a high-performance team, support and synergy among team members, rotational leadership when needed, communication and constant encouragement.

Role efficacy

The performance of people working in an organization depends on their own potential effectiveness, their technical competence, their skills and experience, and the design of the roles they perform in the office.

Role efficacy is the psychological factor underlying role effectiveness.

It depends on how an individual perceives the role and also how the role has been designed. If a role does not allow a person to use her competence, and the individual feels frustrated in the role, effectiveness is likely to be low.

If the role and the individual are effectively integrated, the role efficacy will be higher.

There are ten dimensions of role efficacy:

Centrality (vs. peripherality): If a role occupant feels that the role is significant or central to the organization, the role efficacy is higher. If the role occupant feels the role is insignificant or peripheral, the efficacy will be low. Counselling and coaching may be necessary in such cases.

Integration (vs. distance): If a role provides for the use of the experience, strengths and skills of the occupant, the efficacy will be higher.

Proactivity (vs. reactivity): If a person takes initiative and is proactive, her role efficacy increases. It also depends on how one takes the role and shapes the outcomes.

Creativity (vs. routine): If the role occupant finds opportunities to be innovative and try new ways of solving problems in a role, the efficacy increases.

Inter-role linkage (vs. isolation): If the role occupant perceives the interdependence with others in the organization, receives help and gives help to others, the efficacy increases. If a person feels isolated, the efficacy drops.

Helping relationships (vs. hostility): If no help is given when asked for and there is perception of hostility, the efficacy decreases. On the other hand, a helping relationship enhances efficacy.

Superordination (vs. deprivation): The perception that one's role contributes to some larger entity, or provides opportunity to work for superordinate goals, contributes to high role efficacy.

Influence (vs. powerlessness): Role efficacy increases in proportion to the person's ability to exercise influence in the role.

Personal Growth (vs. stagnation): When a person has opportunities – and perceives them as such – to grow and develop in his or her role, the efficacy increases.

Confrontation (vs. avoidance): If persons avoid problems, the role efficacy decreases and if they confront them to find solutions, the efficacy increases.

The role occupant must work to enhance his or her role efficacy by clearing doubts about the role and the organization must lend a helping hand wherever needed.

Keep evolving

What are you good at? What do you love doing? What is it that gives you contentment? Keep a palm on your heart and choose that activity honestly. Do not choose what others are doing or what you think will make you famous. Choose the activity that you are good at and find genuinely absorbing.

Try to find ways and means to do the activity as often as possible. Go deep into it and learn all the finer points. Develop your skills in the field, be a learner of the deepest level, and master all the skills needed to be the best in the field. Do not compare or compete with anyone else, compete with yourself, and be your best self.

Challenges will come. Overcome those challenges by hard work and matching your skills to meet the challenge. Stretching yourself more and more will take you to newer heights. You will be fully immersed in what you do. You will learn new skills every day. You will grow every day. You will evolve on an ongoing basis. There is no happiness like this.

Keep evolving, keep learning something new all the time. Think differently and be connected to creativity. Read a book, listen to music, paint, watch a movie, write poetry, pen a short story, record a video with a good message – anything meaningful and beautiful enough to engage you with intensity.

Create or immerse yourself in the creation of another mind. You may start with immersing yourself in the creativity of others and gradually learn to be creative in your own way. Do not be in a hurry. People often make the mistake of taking a jump before they are fully ready. Learning an art or a science takes a long time and requires patience and hard work.

You can create your own happiness by voluntarily engaging in activities like helping someone, being kind, expressing gratitude, nurturing social relationships, increasing flow experiences, practicing yoga and meditation, exercising regularly, and savouring life's little pleasures. Choose the activities that you like and practice them regularly.

Flow

One must carefully understand each word of what Mihaly Csikszentmihalyi says about engagement and happiness:

"Happiness is not something that happens. It is not the result of good fortune or random chance. It is not something that money can buy or power command. It does not depend on outside events, but rather on how we interpret them.

"Happiness, in fact, is a condition that must be prepared for, cultivated, and defended privately by each person. People who learn to control inner experience will be able to determine the quality of their lives, which is as close as any one of us can come to being happy.

"The best moments in our lives are not passive, receptive, relaxing times. The best moments usually occur when a person's body or mind is stretched to its limits in a voluntary effort to accomplish something difficult and worthwhile. Optimal experience is thus something that we make happen."

Flow is the psychology of optimal experience. The optimal state of inner experience is one in which there is order in consciousness. During flow, people experience deep enjoyment, creativity, and a total involvement with life.

Csikszentmihalyi adds, "By stretching skills, by reaching toward higher challenges, a person, who has achieved control over psychic energy and has invested it in carefully chosen goals, becomes an increasingly extraordinary individual."

Plateau experience

Abraham Maslow coined and defined the term "plateau experience" as a sort of continuing peak experience that is more voluntary and one that requires a lifetime of long and arduous effort.

Maslow describes the experience, "Such people who appear to be in harmony with their lives often have moments of an extraordinary occurrence called 'peak experiences'. These are profound moments of intense rapture and well-being, along with possibly the awareness of ultimate truth and the unity of all things. Accompanying them is a heightened sense of control over the body and emotions and a wider sense of awareness."

According to Ed Diener, "Psychological wealth includes life satisfaction, the feeling that life is full of meaning, a sense of engagement in interesting activities, the pursuit of important goals, the experience of positive emotional feelings, and a sense of spirituality that connects people to things larger than themselves."

Stress management

Stress is inevitable in a leadership role. The stress may be physical, mental or emotional.

Devote at least an hour in the morning for yoga and meditation. To start with, sit with back straight and eyes closed. Focus on the incoming breath and the outgoing breath at the entrance of your nostrils. Keeping your eyes closed, look at yourself from the top of your head to the tips of the toes.

Go for a forty-to-fifty-minute walk in nature. Find a

quiet place for ten to fifteen minutes of stretching and bending exercises.

Find time for a session of *yoga nidra* during the day. Yoga nidra provides you complete physical, mental and emotional relaxation. It is very simple. You just have to lie down, put the audio on and listen to the instructions with eyes closed.

Do not be argumentative and do not let your anger go beyond control. Take three deep breaths and relax whenever you feel tense.

Have simple food, fruits and plenty of water. Avoid junk food, tea, coffee, cigarettes and alcohol. Have adequate rest and sleep. Have a positive outlook.

Work is love made visible

Work at its best is about connection, engagement, and commitment. Kahlil Gibran calls "work" as "love made visible". He gives beautiful examples of work done with love:

And what is it to work with love?

It is to weave the cloth with threads drawn from your heart, even as if your beloved were to wear that cloth,

It is to build a house with affection, even as if your beloved were to dwell in that house,

It is to sow seeds with tenderness and reap the harvest with joy, even as if your beloved were to eat the fruit.

It is to charge all things you fashion with a breath of your own spirit.

Work is love made visible.

Cultivating a close, warm-hearted feeling for others automatically puts the mind at ease. It helps remove whatever fears or insecurities we may have and gives us the strength to cope with any obstacles we encounter. It is the ultimate source of success in life.

Dalai Lama

HAPPINESS AND WELL-BEING

A ROADMAP FOR A FRUITFUL AND FULFILLING LIFE

"Happiness does not come automatically. It is not a gift that good fortune bestows upon us and a reversal of fortunes takes back. It depends on us alone. One does not become happy overnight, but with patient labour, day after day. Happiness is constructed, and that requires effort and time. In order to become happy, we have to learn how to change ourselves."

Luca and Francesco Cavalli-Sforza

My happiness journey has been truly fulfilling. It has made my life meaningful. I have experienced love, gratitude, forgiveness, kindness, flow, hope, optimism, joy, laughter, well-being, flourishing, yoga, meditation, mindfulness, inner peace, compassion, and equanimity.

I am happy to share below all that I have learned about happiness and well-being. These are, in fact, notes that I have taken. from time to time, while studying the great works of the great minds. I am sure the notes will immensely benefit the readers.

Happiness is the experience of joy, contentment, or positive well-being, combined with a sense that one's life is good, meaningful, and worthwhile.

The five elements of well-being are:

positive emotion,

engagement,

relationships,

meaning,

and accomplishment.

Positive Emotion includes the feelings of joy, excitement, contentment, hope, and warmth. There may be positive emotions relating to the past, present or future.

Engagement denotes deep involvement in a task or activity. One does not experience the passing of time. One experiences flow in sports, music, and singing but one may also experience it in work, reading a book, or in a good conversation.

We feel happy when we are among family and friends. The quality and depth of *relationships* in one's life make it rich.

Meaning is connecting to something larger than life.

One strives for *achievements* in life as a source of happiness.

Each of these elements contributes to well-being. The good news is that each one of the above may be cultivated and developed to enhance the level of well-being.

The Happiness Formula:

H = S + C + V

where H represents the enduring level of happiness, S is the set range, C is the circumstances of life, and V represents the variables under our voluntary control.

The enduring level of happiness is different from momentary happiness. Momentary level of happiness may change with small burst of positive feelings.

Almost 50% of our inherent happiness level is genetic. This means that we can only be as happy as our parents or grandparents. That is the set range of happiness.

Furthermore, there are two barriers to becoming happier forever:

The Happiness Thermostat:

Whether good fortune comes our way or misfortune strikes, the built-in happiness thermostat reverts us to our personal set range.

The Hedonic Treadmill:

This causes you to adapt to good things rapidly. As you accumulate material possessions and accomplishments, your expectations rise.

It is possible, but sometimes impractical, to bring about an increase in happiness level by changing the life circumstances. Only 10% of our happiness depends on the circumstances of life. Let us consider how some circumstances impact happiness:

Money:

Wealth is necessary for life satisfaction but, beyond a certain level, added wealth brings no further life satisfaction. People who, value money more than other goals are less satisfied with their life.

Marriage:

Married people are generally happier than unmarried people.

Health:

Objective health is barely related to happiness; what matters is our subjective perception of how healthy we are. Moderate ill health does not lead to unhappiness, but severe illness does.

Education, Climate, Race, and Gender:

None of them matter much for happiness.

Religion:

Religious people are somewhat more happy and more satisfied with life than nonreligious people.

Place of living:

To be happier, live in a wealthy democracy, not in an impoverished dictatorship.

The good news is that 40% of happiness depends on factors under our voluntary control. If you decide to change them, and make the required efforts in the direction, your level of happiness is likely to increase lastingly.

You can make yourself happier by taking up activities, intentionally and voluntarily, that bring joy and happiness. You can create your own happiness by engaging in exercise, yoga, meditation, helping someone, being kind, expressing gratitude, and savouring life's little pleasures.

Positive emotion contributes towards our happiness and well-being. Gratitude, forgiveness, savouring, mindfulness, optimism, and hope are some of the positive emotions that we can feel. Positive emotion may be about our past, present, or future.

We may feel satisfaction, contentment, fulfilment, pride, or serenity about our past. We may feel joy, ecstasy, calm, zest, ebullience, pleasure, or flow in the present moment. Positive emotion about the future includes hope, optimism, faith, and trust.

One is truly happy is one has positive emotion about the past, present, and future but that does not happen in all cases. Some people may be satisfied with the past, but sour in the present, and pessimistic about the future. There can be several other combinations of positive emotion relating to the past, present or future.

Positive emotion - satisfaction about the past, optimism about the future and happiness in the present - may be enhanced with real effort. Positive psychologists have devised happiness activities to increase positive emotion.

Happiness is like a flowing river, not a stagnant pool. It consists in activity – go for a long walk, exercise, do yoga, meditate, sing, dance, paint, play football, swim, travel, or learn a new skill.

Whatever you do, engage fully. Go deep into it, immerse yourself fully. Just like a musician, who forgets himself, is oblivious of the surroundings and time, and ultimately becomes one with the musical instrument and the music.

Engage deeply – be it play, work, love, or parenting. You will experience flow. When you are in flow – deep into music, play, work, reading, or smiling with your child – oblivious of time and self, you are in a paradise.

Flow is total absorption in an activity - you lose sense of time and self. What more could you ask for when you are fully present, immersed in something worthwhile, and there is an exhilarating feeling of transcendence?

Csikszentmihalyi developed a theory of optimal experience based on the concept of *flow* – the state in which people are so involved in an activity that nothing else seems to matter; the experience itself is so enjoyable that people will do it even at great cost, for the sheer sake of doing it.

Flow is what we feel when we are fully alive, involved with what we do, and in harmony with the environment around us. It is something that happens most easily when we sing, dance, or do sports – but it can happen when we work, read a good book, or have a good conversation.

Flow is the psychology of optimal experience. During flow, people experience deep enjoyment, creativity, and a total involvement with life.

Happy people are good at their friendships, families, and intimate relationships.

Friendships do not just happen, they are made. One prominent psychologist suggests that the magic number is to have three friends or companions you can really count on.

Lyubomirsky says, "Show interest in other people and offer them encouragement. Once a friendship forms, create rituals that allow you to get together and be in touch on a regular basis – a weekly date to go to the gym, a book club, a monthly dinner out, a joint vacation, or a daily e-mail. Be helpful and supportive when your friends need it. Affirm their successes."

One of the secrets of successful marriages is that the partners talk a lot. Happy couples have five positive interactions for every negative one. That means that for every negative statement or behaviour – criticizing, nagging, lecturing – there are five positive ones.

Couples in the happiest relationships bring out the best in each other. They help each other get closer to becoming their "ideal" selves. This is known as the *Michelangelo Effect*.

Go along with your partner to learn a skill – yoga, meditation, or even *zumba*. After coming back, practise it daily with your partner. You will observe that your happiness level goes up.

Choose an activity – hobby or voluntary, charitable work – that you can both do together over the weekends. You will feel happier.

People with strong social support are healthier and live longer. An intriguing analysis of three communities of very long-living people – Sardinians in Italy, Okinawans in Japan, and Seventh Day Adventists in

Loma Linda, California – revealed that they all had five things in common. At the top of the list were "put family first" and "keep socially engaged."

Meaning is an important element of happiness and well-being. You cannot imagine a life of authentic happiness without meaning, or connection to something larger than life.

We derive meaning by developing the best within us and serving something beyond ourselves.

It is our duty to take care of our body and mind. Equally important is the welfare of all other beings around us. Mahatma Gandhi said, "The best way to find your self is to lose yourself in the service of others."

Seligman defines a "meaningful life" in these words: "The meaningful life consists in belonging to and serving something that you believe is bigger than the self, and humanity creates all the positive institutions to allow this: religion, political party, being green, the Boy Scouts, or the family."

We spend a large part of our life working. We are talking of work in a broader context – work in the office or a factory, working as a student (study), raising children and single parenting, working in the fields, and milking cows.

In the modern world, people can find goals and flow in many settings, but most people find most of their flow, or deep engagement, at work. Thomas Carlyle wrote, "Blessed is he who has found his work; let him ask no other blessedness.

When asked for his recipe for happiness, Sigmund Freud gave a very short but sensible answer, "work and love." It is true that if one finds flow in work, and in relations with other people, one is well on the way toward improving the quality of life.

In Maslow's famous hierarchy of needs, once people have satisfied their physical needs, such as food and safety, they move on to needs for love and then esteem, which is earned mostly through one's work.

People approach their work in one of the three ways: as a job, career, or calling.

Jonathan Haidt describes them, "If you see work as a job, you do it only for money, you look at the clock frequently while dreaming about the weekend ahead, and you probably pursue hobbies, which satisfy your effectance needs more thoroughly than does your work.

"If you see your work as a career, you have larger goals of advancement, promotion, and prestige. The pursuit of these goals energizes you and you sometimes take work home with you because you want to get the job done properly. Yet, at times, you wonder why you work so hard.

"If you see your work as a calling, however, you find your work intrinsically fulfilling – you are not doing it to achieve something else. You see your work as contributing to the greater good or as playing a role in some larger enterprise the worth of which seems obvious to you."

Csikszentmihalyi observes, "Occasionally cultures evolve in such a way as to make every day productive chores as close to flow activities as possible. There are groups in which both work and family life are challenging yet harmoniously integrated.

"The most striking feature of such places is that those who live there seldom distinguish work from free time. It could be said that they work sixteen hours a day each day, but then it could also be argued that they never work."

Leo Tolstoy wrote, "One can live magnificently in this world if one knows how to work and how to love, to work for the person one loves and to love one's work."

Accomplishment is also an element of well-being. Achieving your goals in life brings happiness. Deep absorption in an activity brings achievement. The winning habit can be a motivation, a pleasurable feeling, and a source of happiness. When one looks back at one's life, he feels happy about his achievements.

Authentic happiness comes from identifying and cultivating your most fundamental strengths and using them every day in work, love, play, and parenting.

By identifying the very best in ourselves, we can improve the world around us, and achieve new and sustainable levels of authentic contentment, gratification, and meaning.

Every major religious and cultural tradition endorses six virtues:

wisdom and knowledge,

courage,

love and humanity,

justice,

temperance,

and spirituality and transcendence.

Happiness is nothing else but virtues in action. There are several distinct routes to each of the six virtues. Signature strengths are the routes – the strengths of character – by which we achieve the virtues. If you want to be happy, you have to discover your signature strengths and put them into action.

The routes to achieve the virtue of wisdom and knowledge are curiosity or interest in the world, love of learning, critical thinking, open-mindedness, ingenuity, originality, practical intelligence, social intelligence, personal intelligence, emotional intelligence, and perspective.

The routes to courage are valour and bravery, perseverance, industry, diligence, integrity, genuineness, and honesty.

Kindness, generosity, loving, and allowing to be loved are the routes to the virtue of humanity and love.

The virtue of justice is attained through citizenship, duty, teamwork, loyalty, fairness, equity, and leadership.

Temperance may be achieved by self-control, prudence, discretion, caution, humility, and modesty.

Transcendence may be reached by practising gratitude, optimism, spirituality, religiousness, faith, sense of purpose, forgiveness, mercy, and appreciation of beauty and excellence. Playfulness, humour, zest, passion, and enthusiasm are also routes to transcendence.

VIA (values in action) *survey of character strengths* helps determine the highest strengths you have. The signature strengths, when used often, enable you to increase the amount of flourishing in your own life and on the planet.

Building strengths and virtues and using them in daily life are very much a matter of making choices. Building strength and virtue is not about learning, training, or conditioning, but about discovery, creation, and ownership.

A life that successfully pursues the positive emotions

about the past, present and future may be called a *pleasant life*.

The *good life* is using your signature strengths to obtain abundant gratification in the main realms of life.

A meaningful life is a life of meaning and comes from using your signature strengths and virtues in the service of something much larger than you are.

To live all three lives is to lead a *full life.*

50% of happiness is in our genes, 10% depends on the circumstances of life, and the rest 40% can be cultivated by us by taking up activities, intentionally and voluntarily, that bring joy and happiness. These intentional activities we called *Happiness Activities.*

You can create your own happiness by engaging in exercise, yoga, meditation, helping someone, being kind, expressing gratitude, and savouring life's little pleasures.

Happiness activities like expressing gratitude, nurturing social relationships, and increasing flow experiences are known to increase your level of happiness. Choose the activities that you like and practice them regularly. You will feel happier.

Here are some evidence-based, scientifically proven, exercises that make you happier:

What-Went-Well:

Each night before going to sleep, write down three things that went well during the day, that made you happy or things for which you are grateful.

These may be small things or important ones.

Doing this exercise regularly can help you appreciate the positive in your life rather than take it for granted.

You can do this exercise on our own or with a loved one - a partner, child, parent, sibling, or close friend.

Expressing gratitude together can contribute in a meaningful way to the relationship.

Have A Beautiful Day:

Set aside a free day every month to indulge in your favourite pleasures.

Pamper yourself.

Have a beautiful day.

Design, in writing, what you will do from hour to hour.

Be mindful and savour every moment of the beautiful day.

Do not let the bustle of life interfere and carry out the plan.

The Gratitude Visit:

Select one important person from your past who has

made a major positive difference in your life and whom you have never fully expressed your thanks.

Take your time to compose a testimonial just long enough to cover one laminated page.

Travel to that person's home.

It is important to do this face to face, not just in writing or on the phone.

Do not tell the person the purpose of the visit in advance; a simple "I just want to see you" will suffice.

When all settles down, read your testimonial aloud slowly, with expression, and with eye contact.

Then let the other person react unhurriedly.

Reminisce together about the concrete events that make this person so important to you.

Gratitude helps us build new relationships and strengthen existing ones.

It dissolves anger, bitterness, and jealousy.

Gratitude is a meta strategy for happiness.

Cultivate an attitude of gratitude to be happier in life.

Simplify:

Answer the following questions -

Where can I simplify?

What can I give up?

Am I spending too much time on the internet or

watching TV?

Can I reduce the number of meetings at work or the duration of some of the meetings?

Am I saying "yes" to activities to which I can say "no"?

Commit to reducing the busyness in your life.

Simplify, slow down, be kind. And do not forget to have an art in your life – music, paintings, theatre, dance, and sunsets.

Practicing Acts of Kindness:

True happiness consists in making others happy.

In our daily lives, we all perform acts of kindness for others.

These acts may be large or small and the person for whom the act is performed may or may not be aware of the act.

Examples include feeding a stranger, donating blood, helping a friend with homework, visiting an elderly relative, or writing a thank-you letter.

Over the next week, try to perform at least three acts of kindness that you may decide.

Learning to Forgive:

This exercise involves letting go of your anger, bitterness, and blame by writing, but not sending a letter of forgiveness to a person who has hurt or wronged you.

In it describe in detail the injury or offence that was done to you.

Illustrate how you were affected by it at the time and how you continue to be hurt by it.

State what you wish the other person had done instead.

End with an explicit statement of forgiveness and understanding: for example, "I realize now that what you did was the best you could at the time, and I forgive you".

Taking Care of your Body and Soul:

Taking care of the body and soul is of utmost importance for happiness and well-being.

Everyone knows that physical exercise is good for health. But positive psychologists have discovered that physical exercise enhances your level of happiness and well-being.

Go for long walks, trek, jog, gym, practice yoga, swim, play basketball, or learn the martial arts. It will not only improve your health and fitness, but it is also good for your overall well-being.

Exercise reduces depression, anxiety, stress, and panic; it betters mental processing, creates longer life, improves sleep quality, and strengthens the immune system.

Research demonstrates that exercise may be the most reliable happiness booster of all activities.

Acting like a happy person also makes you happy - seems strange but it is now scientifically proven. So, go join a laughter club and laugh for no reason. The body cannot differentiate between real and fake laughter and you get an instant mood boost.

Meditation relaxes the body and mind and brings peace. It takes care of your mind, body, and soul. When you are relaxed and peaceful, there is no tension of mind and no tension of body. You are fully stress free and can concentrate upon whatever you do.

Scientists have also found that practising religion and spirituality makes one happy. You may have your own ways of prayers, meditation, or any other rituals.

Overthinking and stress are harmful for your health and reduce your happiness.

Overthinking is thinking too much, needlessly, passively, endlessly, and excessively pondering the meanings, causes, and consequences of your character, your feelings, and your problems. If you want to be happy, avoid overthinking and social comparisons.

"Finish each day and be done with it. You have done what you could; some blunders and absurdities have crept in; forget them as soon as you can. Tomorrow is a new day; you shall begin it serenely and with so high a spirit to be encumbered with your old nonsense," recommends Ralph Waldo Emerson.

Stress is a major contributing factor in lifestyle diseases. Choose stress management techniques like mindfulness of breathing, vipassana or transcendental meditation for coping with stress.

Savour the positive experiences in your life. Benjamin Franklin was right when he said, "Happiness consists more in small conveniences or pleasures that occur every day, than in great pieces of good fortune that happen but seldom."

Have an optimistic approach about future to be happy. Looking at the bright side, finding the silver lining in the cloud, noticing what is right rather than focussing on what is wrong, having positive friends and avoiding the negative ones, giving yourself the benefit of doubt, feeling good about your future and future of the world, or simply trusting that you can get through the day - all are strategies for cultivating optimism.

Do not spend your free time mindlessly. Choose an active pursuit of happiness over passive hedonism. Instead of doing nothing, watching TV, after returning from work, turn to your hobbies, or other activities that challenge you. You may also think of spending quality time with your near and dear ones, finding time to call upon someone not keeping well, or having an engaging conversation with old friends.

Happiness Mantra:

Get up an hour before sunrise.

Go for an early morning walk in nature.

Do some stretching and bending exercises.

Practice yoga and meditation.

Observe silence in the morning hours.

Smile and be kind to all.

Spend quality time with family and friends.

Engage deeply in work, study, play, love, and parenting.

Connect with a meaningful cause.

Health is not just absence of disease. For good health, the joints, muscles, cells, nerves, glands, and each system of the body must be in a state of perfect balance and harmony.

Yoga builds perfect equilibrium of the body, mind, intellect, and soul.

"Yoga is the control of the patterns of consciousness," says sage Patanjali in the *yoga sutras*.

It is generally believed that yoga is a set of stretching, bending, and breathing exercises, which is not true.

Yoga is a way of life leading to holistic health, happiness, and harmony of mind, body, and soul.

Yoga minimizes the impact of stress on the individual. The regular practice of asanas, pranayama, and dhyana strengthens the nervous system and helps people face stressful situations positively.

Yoga can do wonders for your health by stimulating endocrinal systems and taking care of neuro-muscular systems. It is suitable for modern day lifestyle diseases and brings about body-mind union.

Most people think of yoga as asanas only, as a way of physical exercise. Some people think of yoga as postures and breathing exercise. Few know of yoga as a technique of meditation.

Yoga, in fact, is a technique of developing awareness of mind with a view to enjoy life with fullness. The benefit that comes to the body is incidental.

According to Hasmukh Adhia, "While both physical exercise and asana improve our skeleto-muscular, cardio-respiratory, and circulatory systems of the body, yogasana also improves the neuro-muscular system and endocrinal system which control our sympathetic and parasympathetic reactions in case of perceived stress."

Yoga asanas give spectacular results in lifestyle-related diseases such as hypertension, diabetes, anxiety, and depression.

B K S Iyengar says, "Yoga is for everyone. There are asanas to suit every constitution, irrespective of age or physical condition."

By the practice of the parts of yoga impurity (of the mind) diminishes until the rise of spiritual knowledge culminates in (true) awareness of reality.

There are eight parts of yoga discipline:

1. *Yama*: self-restraints

2. *Niyama*: fixed rules

3. *Asana*: postures

4. *Pranayama*: breath control

5. *Pratyahara*: withdrawal

6. *Dharana*: concentration

7. *Dhyana*: meditation

8. *Samadhi*: samadhi

The Five Yamas:

Non-violence, truth, honesty, sensual abstinence, and non-possessiveness.

The Five Niyamas:

Cleanliness, contentment, austerity, self-study, and surrender to God.

Asana:

Steady and comfortable should be the posture.

Pranayama:

The asana having been done, pranayama is the cessation of the movement of inhalation and exhalation. Fitness of the mind for concentration develops through pranayama.

Pratyahara:

Pratyahara is, as it were, the imitation by the senses of the mind by withdrawing them from their respective objects. There is highest mastery over the sense organs by pratyahara.

Dharana:

Concentration (dharana) is binding the mind to one place.

Dhyana:

Uninterrupted stream of the content of consciousness is Dhyana.

Samadhi:

That state (of dharana and dhyana) becomes samadhi when there is only the object appearing without the consciousness of one's self.

Samyama:

The three (dharana, dhyana, and samadhi) together constitute samyama. By mastering it the higher consciousness dawns.

Asana means a state of being in which one can remain physically and mentally steady, calm, quiet, and comfortable.

According to *Hatha Yoga Pradipika*, "Prior to everything, asana is spoken of as the first part of hatha yoga. Having done asana, one attains steadiness of body and mind, freedom from disease and lightness of the limbs."

Regular practice of asana maintains the physical body in an optimum condition and releases the dormant energy potential which is experienced as increased confidence in all areas of life.

It is not correct to think of yoga asanas as a form of exercise. They are essentially techniques for placing the physical body in positions that cultivate awareness, relaxation, concentration, and meditation.

Performed properly, the asanas bring the respiration and metabolism rates down, the consumption of oxygen and the body temperature drop. During exercise, the breath and metabolism speed up, oxygen consumption rises, and the body gets hot.

Modern day diseases are most lifestyle diseases that are psychosomatic in nature. When asanas are performed correctly, they relax the mind, tone up the autonomic nerves, hormonal functions, and the activities of internal organs.

The asanas are classified into three groups: beginners, intermediate, and advanced.

The beginners' group must be performed by those who have never practised asanas before. The intermediate group consists of asanas which are reasonably difficult and are recommended for people who can perform the beginners' group comfortably. The advanced group is meant for people with good control over their muscles and nervous system, who have already mastered the middle group of asanas.

One should begin one's practice with *chaalan kriya*, or *sookshma vyayam*, or the subtle exercises. This group of asanas facilitates releasing tensions from the body, strengthening the digestive system, and improving the energy flow within the body. Exercises for the eyes may also be added here.

Within the beginners' group, you have asanas that may be performed while standing, sitting, or lying down. Then you have the relaxation asanas and the meditation asanas. It is recommended to include a suitable and balanced mix of these postures in your daily routine.

The intermediate group includes forward and backward bending postures, spinal twisting asanas, inverted asanas, and balancing asanas.

The practices in the advanced group require the limbs and joints to move into unusual positions to which they are not habituated. These asanas are designed to further improve the health of already healthy persons and not for therapeutic purposes. These asanas strongly affect the energy of the body.

Early morning is the ideal time for the practice of asanas. If you are choosing any other time, ensure a gap of at least three to four hours after meals.

Breathing should be done through the nose, unless specifically instructed to do otherwise. Be aware of the posture, breath, and sensations felt in the body while performing the asana.

Never exert undue force and do not stay in the asana if discomfort is experienced. Observe the contra-indications given for the asanas carefully. It is advisable to practice under the guidance of a yoga teacher initially.

Asanas make your body supple, sharpen alertness of your mind, and maintain a physical, physiological, and emotional balance.

B K S Iyengar says, "The practice of asanas lubricates joints, and increases mobility, bringing about an awareness of each muscle, joint, and organ.

"Asanas are based on the simple principles of stretching, bending, rotating, and relaxing. These movements have diverse effects on the body's systems, and will either heal, stimulate, or seal off specific parts of the body.

"At the same time, the approach is holistic, aimed at purifying and strengthening each organ, bone, and cell of the body."

The practice of asanas also increases our ability to bear pain. The energy that is otherwise dissipated in coping with stress and pain is diverted to healing, as the mind is calm and relaxed.

The ancient yogis used logs of wood, stones, and ropes to help them practise asanas effectively. Yogacharya B K S Iyengar invented props which allow asanas to be held easily and for a longer duration, without strain.

A yoga prop is any object that helps to stretch, strengthen, relax, or improve the alignment of the body. Students of yoga find the practice of asanas with props a very encouraging exercise.

Iyengar says, "I have found that even those in good condition occasionally find some poses difficult to sustain for the required length of time. Some asanas, too, entail body movements that are initially too complicated for even the healthiest students to attempt without help.

"With these props, the practice of asanas has never been easier, less tiring, or more enjoyable, making each asana equally accessible to all yoga students."

Asanas practised with the help of props have been found to be useful to relieve many common ailments, and remove stiffness in the back, hips, knees, and feet.

The commonly used props include chair, stool, bench, bolster, block, blanket, crepe bandage, yoga belt, and yoga wheel.

One may also take the support of a wall to help maintain balance and a sense of alignment while performing standing and inverted asanas.

Surya Namaskara is almost a complete sadhana, containing asana, pranayama and meditational techniques within the main structure of the practice. It also has the depth and completeness of a spiritual practice.

Surya means 'sun' and namaskara means 'salutation'. Surya namaskara may be translated as 'salutations to the sun'.

Surya namaskara is a well-known and vital technique within the yogic repertoire. It is a practice which has been handed down from the sages of vedic times.

It is a technique of solar vitalization, a series of exercises which recharge us like a battery, enabling us to live more fully and joyfully with dynamism and skill in action.

Surya namaskara is an effective way of loosening up, stretching, massaging and toning all the joints, muscles and internal organs of the body. Its versatility and application make it one of the most useful methods of inducing a healthy, vigorous and active life, while at the same time preparing for spiritual awakening and the resulting expansion of awareness.

Surya namaskara is a series of twelve physical postures. These alternate backward and forward bending asanas flex and stretch the spinal column and limbs through their maximum range. The series gives such a profound stretch to the whole body that few other forms of exercise can be compared with it.

Surya namaskara can be easily integrated into our daily lives as it requires only five to fifteen minutes' practice daily to obtain beneficial results remarkably quickly.

The five Tibetan rites of rejuvenation, or simply, *The Five Tibetans*, are five yogic exercises practiced by the Tibetan lamas in the Himalayas. These five dynamic exercises enhance health, energy, and vitality.

The five yogic exercises are reputed to strengthen the body, regenerate the mind, and stem the aging process. Regular practice of these postures, tunes and energizes the chakras, and leads to deep relaxation and well-being.

They take only a minimum of daily time and effort, but dramatically increase flexibility of the body as well as mental sharpness.

People from all age groups can learn and do them easily. And most important, it can be practiced daily without any difficulty.

According to Christopher S. Kilham, "The Five Tibetans stimulate full energy flow through the chakras and enliven corresponding nerves, organs, and glands. These exercises also tone and strengthen the major muscle groups, contributing to a strong, resilient physique."

Yoga Nidra is a systematic method of inducing complete physical, mental, and emotional relaxation. The state of relaxation is reached by turning inwards, away from outer experiences.

It is a more efficient and effective form of psychic and physiological rest and rejuvenation than conventional sleep. A single hour of yoga nidra is as restful as four hours of ordinary sleep.

Yoga nidra means sleep with a trace of consciousness. It is a state of mind in between wakefulness and dream. When you practise yoga nidra, you are opening the deeper phases of your mind. It is a technique which can be used to awaken divine faculties and is one of the ways of entering samadhi.

It is a simple practice. You have just to lie down on your back, close your eyes, and listen to the instructions on the audio. You are required to carry out the instructions mentally as much as you can and not to worry if you do not follow any part of the instructions. The only thing is that you should not sleep during yoga nidra.

Meditation brings peace of mind. It enables us to live our life optimally. It calms the mind; removes anger, hatred, and ignorance; and develops love, compassion, and wisdom.

Deep meditation leads to nibbana – the state of supreme bliss, where you are free from all pain and suffering.

Here is a step-by-step guide for a universal practice of meditation, thousands of years old. The Buddha attained enlightenment practising it and taught it to thousands of people. It is known as *anapanasati,* mindfulness of breathing.

Instructions for practice:

Sit down with legs folded crosswise, back straight, and eyes closed.

Always mindful, breathe in; mindful, breathe out.

Be aware of your breath around your nostrils as you breathe in and as you breathe out.

Breathing in long, understand: I am breathing in long; breathing out long, understand: I am breathing out long.

Breathing in short, understand: I am breathing in short; breathing out short, understand: I am breathing out short.

Do not try to regulate your breath in any way. Observe your natural breath as it is.

Be aware of your body as you breathe in and as you breathe out.

Breathe in experiencing the whole body, breathe out experiencing the whole body.

Breathe in relaxing the whole body, breathe out relaxing the whole body.

Don't worry if your mind wanders away, gently bring it back and observe your breath.

Ever mindful, breathe in; mindful, breathe out.

Be aware of your feelings as you breathe in and as you breathe out.

Breathe in experiencing your feelings, breathe out experiencing your feelings.

Breathe in experiencing rapture, breathe out experiencing rapture.

Breathe in experiencing pleasure, breathe out experiencing pleasure.

Be aware of your mental processes as you breathe in and as you breathe out.

Breathe in experiencing mental formations, breathe out experiencing mental formations.

Breathe in tranquilizing mental formations, breathe out tranquilizing mental formations.

Ever mindful, breathe in; mindful, breathe out.

Be aware of your mind as you breathe in and as you breathe out.

Breathe in experiencing the mind, breathe out experiencing the mind.

Breathe in gladdening the mind, breathe out gladdening the mind.

Breathe in concentrating the mind, breathe out concentrating the mind.

Breathe in liberating the mind, breathe out liberating the mind.

Ever mindful, breathe in; mindful, breathe out.

As you breathe in and as you breathe out, contemplate on the impermanence of physical and mental events.

Breathe in focusing on impermanence, breathe out focusing on impermanence.

As you breathe in and as you breathe out, contemplate on the fading away of formations.

Breathe in focusing on fading away, breathe out focusing on fading away.

As you breathe in and as you breathe out, contemplate on the cessation of suffering.

Breathe in focusing on cessation, breathe out focusing on cessation.

As you breathe in and as you breathe out, contemplate on the giving up of defilements.

Breathe in focusing on relinquishment, breathe out focusing on relinquishment.

Ever mindful, breathe in; mindful, breathe out.

May all beings be happy, be peaceful, be liberated.

Open your eyes and come out of meditation.

Everyone knows that laughter is the best medicine but how many of us have a good dose of laughter every day?

Mirthful laughter generates feel good hormones and busts stress instantly. To reap the benefits of laughter, one needs to laugh deep from the diaphragm for about twenty minutes daily. It expels all the stale air from the body and rejuvenates our lungs with fresh oxygen.

Laughter yoga is a unique laughter delivery system

that enables us to laugh for no reason, without the use of jokes, comedy, or humour, even when the going is not good.

We begin laughter with the aid of laughter exercises that turns infectious through eye contact and child-like playfulness of the participants in the group. The practice of laughter yoga may seem frivolous to a layman, but it has a deep and profound impact upon the practitioners. It works wonders for the immune system and is a powerful cardiovascular exercise.

You must have seen members of laughter clubs giggling and having fun in parks. That is group laughter – a more conducive form of laughter yoga.

It generally starts with some gentle warm-up exercises – stretching, bending, twisting, and yogic breathing.

Laughter yoga routine is designed scientifically to have four steps:

The first step is clapping and chanting *"hoho hahaha"*.

The second step is deep breathing – exhale while bending forward, inhale while raising your arms up. It culminates with holding the breath for a while going up, saying *"hold it- hold it – hold it"* in an ascending voice, and then bending down, tapping thighs, running around saying *"hahaha"*.

The third step is child-like playfulness. A positive

affirmation *"Very Good, Very Good, Yay"* is chanted joyously, clapping, and then opening and throwing the arms upwards.

Then, begin the laughter exercises in the fourth step. These exercises help in triggering laughter, which is then taken forward by the group and everyone laughs whole-heartedly.

Greeting laughter, milkshake laughter, mobile laughter, gradient laughter, hearty laughter, silent laughter, lion laughter, appreciation laughter, argument laughter, Calcutta laughter and tak-jhoom laughter are some of the popular laughter exercises practised in laughter clubs.

Just close your eyes and start laughing gently.

Laughter meditation may be experienced while standing up, sitting down, or lying.

Let laughter take its own course. If you do not feel like laughing, stop. When you again feel like laughing, laugh.

Laughter is movement, meditation requires stillness. Laughter meditation is a beautiful and unique experience.

It is not always possible to laugh in a group. One can laugh alone in the morning for a few minutes and the freshness lingers-on all through the day.

There is a growing body of evidence indicating that spiritual practices are associated with better health and wellbeing. Spiritual strength can help you overcome hardships.

Nurturing and developing your spirituality may be just as important as eating a healthy diet, exercising, and building strong relationships. Taking the time to reconnect with what you find meaningful in life and returning to life's big questions can enhance your own sense of connection with something larger than yourself.

Spirituality may be expressed by working for a noble and worthy cause - taking care of the environment, conservation of wild life, rescuing child labour, educating girl child, feeding hungry ones, and healing those who are suffering from misery and illness.

The aim of spirituality is taking fellow human beings from misery to happiness and creating an environment of world peace and harmony.

The *Dhammapada* is one of the most widely read books on spirituality. Its concise, crystalline verses are a thing of beauty and deep meaning.

It is said in the Dhammapada:

"Abstain from all unwholesome deeds,

Perform wholesome ones,

Purify your mind.

This is the teaching of the Enlightened Ones."

Any action that harms others, that disturbs their peace and harmony is a sinful action, an *unwholesome* action. Any action that helps others, that contributes to their peace and harmony, is a pious action, a *wholesome* action.

There are three types of wrong conduct a human being is capable of: wrong conduct with words, wrong conduct with body, and wrong conduct with mind.

There are four sub-divisions of wrong conduct with words: false speech, slanderous speech, harsh speech. and idle chatter.

Abstaining from false speech: Herein someone avoids false speech and abstains from it. One speaks the truth, is devoted to truth, reliable, worthy of confidence, not a deceiver of people.

Abstaining from slanderous speech: One avoids slanderous speech and abstains from it. What one has heard here one does not repeat there, so as to cause dissension there; and what one has heard there one does not repeat here, so as to cause dissension here.

Abstaining from harsh speech: One avoids harsh language and abstains from it. One speaks such words as are gentle, loving, soothing to the ear; such words as go to the heart, and are courteous, friendly, and agreeable to many.

Abstaining from idle chatter: One avoids idle chatter and abstains from it. One speaks at the right time, in accordance with facts, speaks what is useful, one's speech is like a treasure, uttered at the right moment, accompanied by reason, moderate and full of sense.

There are three sub-divisions of wrong conduct with body – taking life, taking what is not given and sexual misconduct.

Abstaining from the taking of life: Herein someone avoids the taking of life and abstains from it. Without stick or sword, conscientious, full of sympathy, one is desirous of the welfare of all sentient beings.

Abstaining from taking what is not given: One avoids taking what is not given and abstains from it; what another person possesses of goods and property, that he does not take away with thievish intent.

Abstaining from sexual misconduct: One avoids sexual misconduct and abstains from it.

There are three sub-divisions of wrong conduct with mind: covetousness, ill will, and wrong view.

Abstaining from covetousness: Here someone avoids being covetous, one is not a coveter of another's goods and property.

Abstaining from ill-will towards others: One avoids a mind of ill-will and hatred towards other beings.

Abstaining from wrong view: One avoids wrong

view, distorted vision.

There are three types of right conduct a human being is capable of: right conduct with words, right conduct with body, and right conduct with mind.

One can perform wholesome deeds by practising right speech, right action, and right conduct with mind.

Right speech means speaking in ways that are trustworthy, harmonious, comforting, and worth taking to heart. When you make a practice of these positive forms of right speech, your words become a gift to others.

Right action is behaving peacefully and staying in harmony with fellow human beings.

Right mental conduct is having goodwill for others and cultivating the right view.

To purify your mind, you must cultivate wholesome states and abandon unwholesome states by seeking wisdom and practising meditation.

This is the essence of the teachings of the enlightened persons.

In his first sermon, the Buddha expounded the four noble truths and advocated *the middle path*.

He said, "Avoid the two extremes – devotion to pursuit of pleasure in sensual desires and devotion to self-mortification.

"The middle way discovered by the Perfect One gives vision, gives knowledge, and leads to peace, to direct knowledge, to enlightenment, to Nibbana.

"The middle way is the noble eightfold path - right view, right intention; right speech, right action, right livelihood; right effort, right mindfulness, right concentration."

The Four Noble Truths constitute the basic doctrine of the Buddha's teachings.

The first noble truth diagnoses that there is suffering. The second recognizes craving for sensual desires as the root cause of suffering. The third unfolds that there is a way out of this suffering. And the fourth shows the path to the end of all suffering.

The four noble truths are:

Noble Truth of Suffering:

Birth is suffering, aging is suffering, sickness is suffering, death is suffering, sorrow and lamentation, pain, grief, and despair are suffering; association with the loathed is suffering, dissociation from the loved is suffering, not to get what one wants is suffering; in brief, the five aggregates subject to clinging are suffering.

Noble Truth of Origin of Suffering:

The origin of suffering is the craving for sensual desires. It is this craving that leads to renewed existence, accompanied by delight and lust, seeking delight here and there; that is, craving for sensual pleasures, craving for existence, craving for extermination.

Noble Truth of the Cessation of Suffering:

Cessation of suffering is giving up, relinquishing, letting go and rejecting, of craving. It is the remainderless fading away and cessation of that same craving, the giving up, and relinquishing of it, freedom from it, nonattachment.

Noble Truth of the Way Leading to the Cessation of Suffering:

The way leading to cessation of suffering is the Noble Eightfold Path – that is, right view, right intention; right speech, right action, right livelihood; right effort, right mindfulness, right concentration.

The first noble truth points out that the five aggregates subject to clinging are suffering.

The five aggregates subject to clinging are: the form aggregate subject to clinging, the feeling aggregate subject to clinging, the perception aggregate subject to clinging, the volitional or mental formations aggregate of clinging, and the consciousness aggregate of clinging.

The form aggregate includes whatever kind of form there is – whether, past, future, or present, internal or external, gross or subtle, inferior or superior, far or near: this is called the form aggregate.

Likewise, the feeling aggregate, perception aggregate, volitional formations aggregate, and consciousness aggregate are similarly constituted.

These five aggregates are rooted in desire.

One must understand that these five aggregates are impermanent, nonself, and subject to change. In brief, the five aggregates subject to clinging are suffering.

When one sees thus, the mind becomes dispassionate and is liberated from the taints by nonclinging.

One must develop an understanding of the Four Noble Truths.

The noble truth of suffering is to be fully understood.

The noble truth of the origin of suffering is to be abandoned.

The noble truth of the cessation of suffering is to be realized.

The noble truth of the way leading to the cessation of suffering is to be developed.

The Buddha discovered the Four Noble Truths and the Noble Eightfold Path. Both are inter-twined. The four noble truths are the doctrine part, to be understood, and the noble eightfold path is the discipline part, to be practised.

The pathway to the end of suffering is the Noble Eightfold Path. It is that middle way awakened to by the Tathagata, which gives rise to vision, which gives rise to knowledge, and leads to peace, to direct knowledge, to enlightenment, to Nibbana.

The *noble eightfold path* is:

right view,

right intention,

right speech,

right action,

right livelihood,

right effort,

right mindfulness,

and right concentration.

The eight path factors can be divided into three groups:

the *moral discipline* group, consisting of right speech, right action, and right livelihood,

the *concentration* group, consisting right effort, right mindfulness, and right concentration,

and the *wisdom* group, consisting of right view and right intention.

Right View:

Right view is knowledge of suffering, knowledge of

the origin of suffering, knowledge of the cessation of suffering, and knowledge of the way leading to the cessation of suffering.

If we hold a wrong view, it will lead us to wrong action and, eventually, suffering. On the other hand, if we adopt a right view, it will steer us towards right action, and thereby towards freedom from suffering.

The ten courses of unwholesome action are:

Bodily action

Destroying life, taking what is not given, wrong conduct in regard to sense pleasures.

Verbal action

False speech, slanderous speech, harsh speech, idle chatter.

Mental action

Covetousness, ill will, wrong view.

The ten courses of wholesome action are the opposite of these.

The roots of unwholesome action are greed, hatred, and delusion. The three wholesome roots are their opposites.

A wrong view leads to actions that cause hurt and harm to others. A wrong view gives rise to hateful speech and ill will towards others. Unwholesome mental states and speech result in wrong actions causing misery and suffering to oneself and others.

For a person who holds a wrong view, his deeds and words will lead to suffering, while for a person who holds a right view, his deeds and words will lead to happiness.

For a person of wrong view, whatever bodily, verbal, and mental action he undertakes, all lead to harm and suffering. Because the view is bad.

Suppose a seed of bitter gourd were planted in moist soil. Whatever nutrients it would take up from the soil and from the water would all lead to its bitter taste. Because the seed is bad.

For a person of right view, whatever bodily, verbal, and mental action he undertakes, all lead to well-being and happiness. Because the view is good.

Suppose a seed of sugar cane were planted in moist soil. Whatever nutrients it would take up from the soil and from the water would all lead to its sweet taste. Because the seed is good.

The right view leading to the end of suffering, Nibbana, is the understanding of the Four Noble Truths.

Right Intention:

Right intention is intention of renunciation, intention of non-ill will, and intention of harmlessness.

When intentions are right, the actions will be right.

Whenever thoughts of desire, ill will and harmfulness arise in mind, they lead to harm for oneself and others.

Desire is the root of suffering.

Renunciation means turning away from craving, letting go of attachment, not necessarily relinquishing the household.

The intention of good will opposes the intention of ill will, thoughts governed by anger and aversion. The remedy to ill will is generating a heart of loving-kindness for all beings.

The intention of harmlessness is thought guided to compassion. It is the opposite of cruel, aggressive, and violent thoughts. Both, loving-kindness, and compassion, may be developed through the practice of meditation.

Whenever thoughts of desire, ill will, and harmfulness arise in the mind, they lead to harm for oneself and others.

Whenever thoughts of renunciation, goodwill, and harmlessness arise, they are beneficial, conducive to the growth of wisdom, and lead one to the path of Nibbana.

Right Speech:

Right speech is abstinence from false speech, abstinence from malicious speech, abstinence from harsh speech, and abstinence from idle chatter.

One must not speak lies and half-truth. One must

not speak with an intention to bring disrepute to the other person. One must not use offensive words. One must not indulge in gossip that brings no good.

One must speak in way that brings peace and harmony, that creates warmth and love, and that brings a feeling of fearlessness and safety among people.

The four kinds of verbal misconduct are – false speech, divisive speech, harsh speech, and idle chatter.

The roots of these are threefold – greed, hatred, and ignorance.

One who has no shame in speaking lies is empty of spiritual achievement. One who tells a deliberate lie, discards whatever spiritual achievement he has made. One should not speak a deliberate lie even in jest.

Lying is disruptive to social cohesion, slanderous speech is speech intended to create enmity and division, harsh speech causes hurt and pain, and idle chatter stirs up the defilements in one's own mind and in others.

The four kinds of verbal good conduct are – truthful speech, non-divisive speech, gentle speech, and judicious speech.

Right Action:

Right action is abstinence from the destruction of

life, abstinence from taking what is not given, and abstinence from sexual misconduct.

One must not harm other beings. One must not indulge in any form of violence. One must not try to acquire forcibly or by deceit what does not belong to one. One must not indulge in immoral and inappropriate behaviour.

One must abstain from killing any sentient being as all beings love life, seek happiness, tremble at pain and punishment, and fear death. On the contrary, we must develop kindness and compassion towards all beings.

Abstaining from taking what is not given includes abstaining from stealing, robbery, snatching, and acquiring wealth by fraudulent and deceitful means. One must respect the belongings of others.

Abstaining from sexual misconduct implies responsibility and commitment in one's marital and other interpersonal relationships.

Right Livelihood:

Right livelihood is abandoning of wrong mode of livelihood and earning living by a right livelihood.

One must earn livelihood righteously by hard work, by fair means, and not resorting to practices that bring harm to others. Some activities like dealing in intoxicants, weapons, and poison can only cause harm to others. Any other activity that is potentially harmful for the society must be avoided as a means of living.

"These five trades, O monks, should not be taken up by a lay follower: trading in weapons, trading in living beings, trading in meat, trading in intoxicants, trading in poison."

Right Effort:

Right effort is endeavour to prevent unwholesome mental states and arouse wholesome ones.

The five hindrances – sensual desires, ill will, dullness and drowsiness, restlessness and worry, and doubt – are defilements of the mind that come in the way of concentration.

Effort and energy are required to overcome these hindrances and cultivate the mind. The starting point is the defiled mind, and the goal is the liberated mind, purified and illuminated by wisdom.

One abandons, dispels, eliminates, and abolishes gross impurities, namely bad conduct of body, speech, and mind.

Right effort involves the development of wholesome states of mind, like serenity and insight, and nurturing them. It also involves keeping unwholesome states away and reducing defilements on a continuous basis.

Right Mindfulness:

Right mindfulness is contemplation of the body, feelings, mind, and phenomena.

Mindfulness is the presence of mind, attentiveness, or awareness. It facilitates the achievement of both serenity and insight.

Right mindfulness is cultivated through the practice of the four foundations of mindfulness, the mindful contemplation of body, feelings, states of mind, and phenomena.

The Buddha says that the four foundations of mindfulness form the only way that leads to the attainment of purity, to the overcoming of sorrow, and the realization of Nibbana.

Right Concentration:

Right concentration is seclusion from sensual desires and entering upon and abiding in the four meditative states.

Concentration is one-pointedness of mind. It is not attained all at once but develops in stages.

It can be developed through development of serenity or development of insight.

The four sublime states or divine abodes – loving kindness, compassion, sympathetic joy, and equanimity – are the objective bases for deep levels of absorption.

The attainment of concentration makes the mind still, opens vast vistas of bliss, and serenity.

"May all creatures, all living things,

all beings one and all,

experience good fortune only.

May they not fall into harm."

Loving kindness is the desire for the welfare and happiness of all beings. The practice of loving kindness meditation cultivates the feelings of friendliness, goodwill, and non-violence in one's heart and dispels anger, hatred, and negativity.

Loving kindness, compassion, altruistic joy, and equanimity are known as the four divine abodes. These are sublime and noble qualities of love and the ideal way of dealing with all living beings.

These sublime qualities of love provide the answer to all situations we may encounter in our lives. They are the great removers of tension, the great peacemakers in social conflict, and the great healers of wounds suffered in the struggle of existence.

These four states have the potential to purify the heart and create positive energy. Undesirable qualities such as delusion, greed, self-centeredness, and negativity are transformed. States of anger, hatred, loneliness, sorrow, and unhealthy attachments are healed.

There are meditation practices to cultivate the virtues of loving kindness, compassion, altruistic joy, and equanimity. The four divine abodes complement well the mindfulness of breathing technique.

In meditation, there are two basic methods: practices that develop the *head* aspects such as analysis and concentration, and practices that open the *heart*. Both head and heart skills are needed.

Loving kindness is the desire for the welfare and happiness of all beings. It includes friendliness, goodwill, benevolence, fellowship, amity, concord, inoffensiveness, and non-violence.

It is the pure, spiritual, and selfless love of a mother for her only child:

"Even as a mother protects with her life,

Her child, her only child,

So, with a boundless heart

Should one cherish all living beings."

The practice of loving kindness meditation is deep and profound. It comes from a pure and compassionate heart that has no trace of malice inside.

It is a complete practice by itself. It may also complement other meditative practices like the mindfulness of breath and insight meditation.

Cultivating Loving Kindness:

One sits in a secluded place, legs folded crosswise, back straight, and cultivates the thoughts of loving kindness in his mind:

"May all be well and secure,

May all beings be happy!

Whatever living creatures there be,

Without exception, weak or strong,

Long, huge, or middle-sized,

Or short, minute, or bulky,

Whether visible or invisible,

And those living far or near,

The born and those seeking birth,

May all beings be happy!"

The feelings of anger, hatred, and negativity are quite common in people. One may overcome these feelings temporarily, but they rise again at the smallest provocation.

When we cultivate feelings of loving kindness, compassion, altruistic love, and equanimity towards people, our hearts become kinder and warmer. The negative feelings start diminishing gradually, and our hearts start filling with positive feelings.

Meditating on the four divine abodes leads us to sending love and compassion to all living beings – in all directions. We wish happiness for all beings in the sky, earth, and water. We pray that no living being, small or big, may suffer in any way.

There remain no feelings of harm, hatred, or violence. There is only love, compassion, and good will. One feels calm and the mind is full of peace.

When the mind is tranquil, and devoid of any unwholesome states, one is lead to higher states of consciousness.

You may practice any type of meditation you prefer, but towards the end, when the mind is still, devote a few minutes to cultivating loving peace and compassion for the universe and its beings.

"All the joy the world contains,

Has come through wishing happiness for others.

All the misery the world contains,

Has come through wanting pleasure for oneself."

Shanti Deva

EPILOGUE

AUTHETIC LEADERSHIP TO
AUTHENTIC HAPPINESS

"Winners
don't do
different things.
They do things
Differently."
Shiv Khera

Know thyself.

Be kind to people.

Lead from your heart.

Be authentic.

Be happy.

Flourish!

> "That is happiness –
> to be dissolved
> into something
> complete and great."
> Willa Cather

REFERENCE
BOOKS

Born to Win:

Transactional Analysis with Gestalt Experiments

By Muriel James and Dorothy Jongeward

Games People Play:

The Basic Handbook of Transactional Analysis

By Eric Berne

I'm OK – You're OK:

The Transactional Analysis Breakthrough

That's Changing the Consciousness

and Behaviour of People Who

Never Before Felt OK About Themselves

By Thomas A. Harris

Staying OK
By Amy Bjork Harris
and Thomas A. Harris

Theories and Models in Applied Behavioral Science:
Volume 1: Individual
Edited by J. William Pfeiffer

Theories and Models in Applied Behavioral Science:
Volume 2: Dyads, Groups, Training & Learning
Edited by J. William Pfeiffer

Theories and Models in Applied Behavioral Science:
Volume 3: Management/Leadership
Edited by J. William Pfeiffer

Theories and Models in Applied Behavioral Science:
Volume 4: Organizational
Edited by J. William Pfeiffer

You Can Negotiate Anything:
The World's Best Negotiator
Tells You How to Get What You Want

By Herb Cohen

Don't Say YES When You Want To Say NO:
The Assertiveness Training Book
By Herbert Fensterheim
and Jean Baer

Emotional Intelligence:
Why It Can Matter More Than IQ
By Daniel Goleman

Working with Emotional Intelligence
By Daniel Goleman

Focus:
The Hidden Driver of Excellence
By Daniel Goleman

Lateral Thinking
By Edward de Bono

Six Thinking Hats
By Edward de Bono

The Seven Habits of Highly Effective People:

Powerful Lessons in Personal Change
By Stephen R. Covey

First Things First
By Stephen R. Covey
and A. Roger Merrill
with Rebecca R. Merrill

A Theory of Human Motivation
By A. H. Maslow

How to Win Friends and Influence People
By Dale Carnegie

You Can Win
By Shiv Khera

Happiness:
A Guide to Developing Life's Most Important Skill
By Matthieu Ricard

Authentic Happiness:
Using the New Positive Psychology to
Realize Your Potential for Lasting Fulfillment

By Martin E. P. Seligman

Flourish:
A New Understanding of Happiness and Well-Being –
and How to Achieve Them
By Martin Seligman

Flow:
The Psychology of Optimal Experience
By Mihaly Csikszentmihalyi

The Happiness Hypothesis:
Finding Modern Truth in Ancient Wisdom
By Jonathan Haidt

The Science of Happiness:
How Our Brains make Us Happy
and What We Can Do to Get Happier
By Stefan Klein

The Happiness Advantage:
The Seven Principles of Positive Psychology
That Fuel Success and Performance at Work
By Shawn Achor

The How of Happiness:
A New Approach to Getting
the Life You Want
By Sonja Lyubomirsky

Happier:
Learn the Secrets to Daily Joy
and Lasting Fulfillment
By Tal Ben-Shahar

Asana Pranayama Mudra Bandha
By Swami Satyananda Saraswati

Yoga:
The Path to Holistic Health
By B. K. S. Iyengar

Surya Namaskara
By Swami Satyananda Saraswati

Yoga Nidra
By Swami Satyananda Saraswati

Laughter Yoga:

Daily Laughter Practices for Health and Happiness
By Dr Madan Kataria

The Art of Meditation
By Matthieu Ricard

The Life of the Buddha
By Bhikkhu Nanamoli

In the Buddha's Words:
An Anthology of Discourses
from the Pali Canon
Edited and introduced by Bhikkhu Bodhi

The Noble Eightfold Path:
Way to the End of Suffering
By Bhikkhu Bodhi

The Dhammapada:
Wisdom of The Buddha
Translated by Max Mueller

ABOUT THE AUTHOR

Jagat Singh Bisht

Happiness Author, Blogger, Laughter Yoga Master Trainer, Behavioural Science Trainer, and Founder: LifeSkills.
Authored seven books on happiness: Cultivating Happiness, Nirvana – The Highest Happiness, Meditate Like the Buddha, Mission Happiness, A Flourishing Life, Positive Education, and The Little Book of Happiness.
He served in a bank for thirty-five years and has been propagating happiness and well-being among people for the past twenty years.
He is on a mission – Mission Happiness!

BOOKS BY THIS AUTHOR

Cultivating Happiness

A GUIDE TO PRACTICES THAT DO WONDERS:
LEARN PRACTICES TO FIND MEANING, PEACE AND WELL-BEING:
You can change your life if you have the right understanding and adopt proven practices for creating happiness.

This is a comprehensive guide on the art of living and the science of being, based on years of study and practical sessions.

It includes a step-by-step guide to twelve sets of exercises and a treasure trove of timeless wisdom.

The book is a unique confluence of positive psychology, laughter yoga, yoga, meditation, and spirituality.

It is the right place for beginners to take the first steps and for the advanced learners to add more skills to their repertoire.

You will experience cheerful health, authentic happiness, and everlasting peace once you adopt these practices.

Mission Happiness

My Idyllic Life:
This is a book on happiness, an autobiography, and a memoir that takes you for a journey on the pathway of authentic happiness, well-being, and a meaningful life. It gives you a new understanding of happiness and well-being and how to achieve them.
It takes a peek at my formative years, my work life, and my experiments with happiness. You will find, inside, a roadmap for a fruitful and fulfilling life, based on years of deep study and practical experience. It blends the best of positive psychology, meditation, yoga, laughter yoga, and spirituality.
The book will enable you to discover new ways to flourish in life, find inner peace, and contribute towards enhancing well-being on this planet. You will gain tremendous insight into life and happiness. The new learning, investigation, and wisdom can catapult you into higher realms of existence!

Nirvana – The Highest Happiness

BE A BUDDHA IN THE MODERN WORLD:
The Buddha taught the Dhamma – the law of nature, the path of truth -about two thousand and five hundred years ago.

A lot of time has since elapsed, and much water has flown down the rivers. The whole world has changed drastically but the guiding principles of spirituality remain the same.

The Buddha understood that this world is in turmoil. There is stress, misery, and pain all around. The human beings are suffering.

After a long struggle for enlightenment, he arrived at the root cause of all suffering, and discovered a path leading to liberation from suffering, to peace, to happiness.

This book helps you to understand Nirvana – the culmination of the quest for perfection and happiness – and takes you on the path leading to Enlightenment.

It presents the Buddha's teachings in a crystalline form and acquaints you with the quintessence of the practice of meditation.

It takes you on the way to the end of suffering, pain, and distress.

If you are seeking a stress-free life, peace of mind, and spiritual wisdom, this book would be of immense benefit.

Meditate Like The Buddha

A STEP-BY-STEP GUIDE:
This is essentially a book for beginning, establishing, strengthening, and consolidating your meditative practice. The instructions are simple and crystal clear.

It is a step-by-step guide for meditation based on practical experience. It explains in detail a universal practice of meditation thousands of years old. The Buddha attained enlightenment practising it and taught it to thousands of people for the next forty-five years. If you seek the serenity of the Buddha, you must learn to meditate like the Buddha.

Meditation calms the mind; removes anger, hatred, and ignorance; and develops love, compassion, and wisdom. It enables us to live our life optimally. Deep meditation leads to Nibbana – the state of supreme bliss, where you are free from all pain and suffering.

It includes supplementary reading material derived from the Pali Canon for gaining insight and spiritual development. This book is a treasure trove for all meditators.

A Flourishing Life

EFFORTLESS PRACTICES FOR HAPPINESS AND STRESS MANAGEMENT:

Do you want to be happier? Would you like to increase your well-being and flourish? This book will help you flourish!

Flourishing is the experience of life going well - a combination of feeling good and functioning effectively. It is the opposite of languishing - living a life that feels hollow and empty.

Everyone seeks a flourishing life, but the modern-day lifestyle generates a lot of stress, which is the cause of psychosomatic disorders, including hypertension, respiratory ailments, gastrointestinal disturbances, migraine, and ulcers.

In this book, you will find simple, effortless, and painless practices for authentic happiness, stress management, and lasting peace. These exercises are easy to do, can be taken up by anyone, and require no previous training or experience.

The contents include how to relax your body and mind, knowing your inner self, freestyle exercise, life-long learning and evolving, autonomy and self-determination, flourishing, and spirituality.

After reading this book, you will have a deep understanding of the elements of authentic happiness and well-being. This book helps you to lead a flourishing life.

Positive Education

Happiness Fundamentals for Children and Parents:

Do you wish to prepare your child with life skills, such as, grit, optimism, resilience, growth mindset, engagement, and mindfulness?

A combination of traditional education with the study of happiness and well-being can be of great help in this regard.

Children and parents can flourish in life by practicing scientifically proven happiness activities.

The concepts are derived from Positive Psychology,

the modern science of happiness and well-being, and Positive Education, an approach that focuses on specific skills that assist students to strengthen their relationships, build positive emotions, enhance personal resilience, promote mindfulness, and encourage a healthy lifestyle.

There are books for children and there are books for the grown-ups. This one is for both of them – the children and their parents. The book may also be used for implementing positive education in schools.

Printed in Great Britain
by Amazon